AF395919

James Loop

Metronome

Winter Editions, 2026

Contents

For Michael

The End

remember me reader
age thirty four and naked
in a small kitchen
straining spaghetti
while reading the aeneid

to what perilous absurdities
of love and nutriment
would I not stoop
out of the hope of you

There

Nocturne

1.

memory licks
as waves may lick
the flesh of a man
bound waist deep
to a post in the sea
away
over a day or two

it's a complicated figure
and belabored with
at least one flawed wheel

he won't disappear

2.

there's a wire
where the spine goes
that radiates a preharmonic music

it pulls the glass and copper beasts
without fear from the forest toward him

a fugitive continuance

his flesh
curious endures

Two Pastorals

1.

—that that drawing
room was really out
of its "mind," what, like
a Sodom-on-Hudson:
the early yard, the pink
paganish sun-rinse
in which (after significant
needling) you acquiesced
and fucked me, yes?

oh, definitive feeling!
dollars of my love!

2.

There once was a faggot named Rose
Who douched with a garden hose
His hole was as clean
As his suitors were mean
And his flowers were dead in their rows

The Devil

what I wanted was something else
everyone says it
a trapdoor in the language
the godhead piano falling then
falling then
to be smashed eloquently under it
bang

being in love is no excuse
not if what is meant by love is what I meant by it
I was running and the road ran out
hadn't I already done that
I know I could have been found
doing something those long years
years stacked like volumes of steam
in the thin library of
                       I lost track
what I wanted was something else to call the fear of wanting
    nothing
I was serious then I was not I tried those
sainthood etc.
or disappearing into an agitated cursive

you'll forgive yourself of anything
if you believe you are in love
okay then belief's out
we shall eat our dinners straight off the table no plates

you know your problem is your ideas
it's not as easy not to have them as having sex or reading books

and anyway you'd never allow yourself a solitude
it's boring we have to be honest
would you chew your own ideas off

would you like a dog who chews its leg off
chew through the ligaments ideal
that bind you like a kite
then an anchor then
like a kite again
to others still
blazing there like tigers always
blazing there like tigers
                    others

Motto

<pre>
  what binds
what breaks
            the river
      makes
            the river
            the river
</pre>

The Alphabet

lucky us as
in its alien shrine
no one, none
boils alone

lucky us as

We All Work in the Hot Dog Factory Now

We all work in the hot dog factory now
Kissing late on the cheek and late to
And already working at work at work
In the hot dog factory we all don't
Eat them and messaging webs the dogs
And us who work at work and working
Worked in the hot dog factory we all
Live in the hot dog lotto hopscotch of
Essential surgeries hot dollars for eating
And working so long in the hot dog lotto
Factory I met my mother and found her
Asked too much of I met my sister there
Rattled hot to the touch we all work in
The hot hot scraped and tensile dogs
Gone to replicating replicator replication
Where we work while we work in the
Hot dog lotto hopscotch hot dog factory

Eating

It started with a man I wanted to eat.

He was into big guys. That's a thing.

He told me, "I have two sexualities: the fantasy one and the
    real world one."

I didn't eat him in either.

So when he vanished I started to grow.

On purpose at first: I bought a white powder, "Mass Gainer,"

Synthesized to be supercaloric.

I found a job selling Christmas trees and got bigger still.

I liked the way my hands looked coated in a thin layer of black
    sap.

I liked the feeling—a new one—of being hungry from a day of
    hard work.

I've never been much at home in my body. It's an old story.

Words instead, like Mishima said, the words

Rotted my body from childhood (paraphrase).

There is something I love to say no to.

You could call it the whole shebang.

Shitting, eating, fucking, dying

Over and over again.

I wish that we could procreate as trees,

Thomas Browne writes that, or something like it.

My swollen hands and sweaty beanie would bring to mind
    my dad

Whose hands are like huge red crab claws from a lifetime
    of work.

Of course when I tell him that, he grows grandiose,

(Just one of the traits I inherited).

I text him a picture of my working hands.

He replies ... well, in fact I don't remember.

Something along the lines of

Be happy you haven't had to work like that every day.

It's true it was mostly a vacation from my informational labor,

To a place called "My Body"—don't you hate that?

When a poet says Body, Body.

Is there anything less sexy, less embodied than that?

The point is I kept eating but returned to my ghoulish inbox job.

I was grieving in an outsize manner.

I wanted there to be a record in the flesh

Or to eat the child I was,

Piece by bloody piece.

A plague of sighing and grief! It blows a man up like a bladder.

That's Falstaff. He's right about that.

I noticed it first on the stairs.

Huffing and puffing I called it.

Then while tying my shoes:

The distance between my hands and feet seemed to have
    increased.

A belly out of nowhere hung there,

Some new continent or planet spun from nothing,

From a brush with nothing.

At first my sexual capital increased in a way that was curious
    to me.

I was Daddy Christmas Tree.

Sure, I can do that.

Then came the chasers.

I thought again of my dad and his large boozy belly.

I thought of the phrase from "Howl,"

"Who purgatoried their torsoes night after night."

When I was younger that sounded erotic.

But I understand now, the pain of climbing the mountain.

Is that poetry I don't care.

I want to be a good writer and an honest man. That's James
    Baldwin.

By now I think I've got the man part down.

I hear him cry.

A History of Style

Rembrandt's Dog

despite her
skeletal wreck best
rendered by the history of art

Mind-Body Problem

a shorn sun lurks loose
in his diagram today

a day he may apply his legs to

snipped clean
at the stem
unbelievably translucent

Love To

       seduce you as if
it were literally
1605

       with many affectionate
verbal profusions & now
& then an
         affectionate
hand on your cock

came he
then to the pig tower

crenels and arrowslits

crisp spires
sliding
into violet gel

the reversal

abracadabra asshole

all doors take wing before him

Celebration

oh good
a treacherous little path
through the dark wood

shall we have a spiritual type of experience?

Lycidas

He was by north and south a slick true lay

He was the extrapolated castaway

He was ah me a matchstick underway

He was what I could say and could not say

Denmark

nests twitch in spruces

villagers glitter
in their season of acuteness

and on a single spasm's archive
swivels
the black night

ideal

nor grace nor ice

Name Day

my thirtieth name day in the market
I can see nothing but plastics
some somber silver fruit feeling eating remembered
blueberries in automatic February
wants traced on the very earth

when I lived I liked to rhyme it
my name's James
and friendship dreamt
enough it was for me

radiant blue sleep starts
to slip from its husk

a people at the lip of weird heat
and worry inflected first as fruit is
usurped sadness its own
eaten ifs

my name not what
the word peeled
from raw rock
and tormented
perfect systems

then we'll be hard past belief
and bear addressing

place our pleasures in a row

nest in each readiness
a split pedagogical fruit
says not the hoped for
but nonetheless
the born one

nonetheless
the one born

Volatility

little sun gold tomatoes
soften in the actual sun's
sudden rented yellow kitchen

and there goes my old mind
tossing them up on musty stage
to sing dissolution chansons

can't you James
let anything be

This is Serious, James

this is serious, James
this time it's for real for real
no more dry runs
nor hesitations
blistered with refinement

the time to panic is now, James
so gather your stomachs into your throat
your human throat
gather them there gather
your he-stomachs and she-stomachs
and make it count

James, this is no drill
no joke's freaked filaments
can be coyly called for now
just you wait and see
or try and call one

it's really the big one this time, James
there's no way out
the wave's come in
the actual floor has cracked in half
and the little sprites and archangels
are truly whizzing now

yes, the moment is finally here, James
so let's see that marvelous fear
unveiled at last
you have been readying all your days

Saturn

1.

could it it could could it it could could it it could
go on forever this way that's not
true it could go on forever this way

even if which it shouldn't it should
not cling
a voice gets all over
itself its offered embrace it offers its
spleen and embrace

that the year may never begin
that the year, a body both
master and pet, a year,
the body-mastery, a pet name,
project intended and intended

oh my garden!
I played a trick on you
told you you should grow that you were asked for that you
        asked for

this
dedicatory epistle: dear
you, it's
I, your
dreadfulest, dear
friends you'll find my face

even if I
should have to remove it leave it
streaming at your feet, even
if I should rub it against your eyes
away

could it it could could it it could
father
be yours

2.

my my my

when I fell I fell
for your latex syntax and tax proposal

you were a sugar

you were   like you could
                like you could

value nothing nor value

a cock like   a sugar
a cock like   a spade

digging   yes daddy
                 I do

3.

I was you said
of very little use and small powers,
arcing deflected surf-light. I touched nothing.

So

        desire: a corpse in the drain,
        beyond blame, discoloring rain.

4.

The drag of history felt as guilt as debt gelds flight.
A gilded doubt is history as debt is guilt and a drag.
Historically doubt as a dab of gall is a gilded dildo,
As history is guilt and the gall all of it.

5.

Picture the moments before you wake. Tunnels cramped and
drawn, corrected bones, the battery light of expectation.

One theory of pain is it's obvious, obviates theory, as in
you're in it or you're not. Imagine a pain.

Wake in imagined pain, in imagery: damp light, centimeters
of birds dredging blues. What's a reason to move? Pain, if
moving might remove it. It may, you do, maybe.

How well do you care for yourself? If you were a dog, how
would you judge the master which is you? Poorly I'm afraid.

Imagine eating. Imagine being eaten: that the matter with
you be converted into energy, into continuing life. That is the
theory, the hope of being eaten. That much is obvious.

Seeing scar tissue you guess at the wound.

6.

A word is a wound on time. Grief, a pleat. It eats
light abdicates and festers: the poem. I tell you:

> *The birch burst like wheel spokes*
> *through a snowed-in closeness.*

Impossibility sees I am like this
to you that I would like to be like this

to you

7.

Under you now I am leaden and heavy
and everyone wants my money. My money
is not enough money. What little there is
I spend unwisely. I a debtor

am and walk with a debtor's signature
gait, extending his guaranteed hand:
Prussian blue PVCA. I make silence
in my free time of varied density and weight

though to write also is faulty accounting.
We're mortgaged by words
which extend themselves not
in a gesture of faith, but because they know

in heaven all bills get paid. Someone would eat
your pain I say though I say neither I nor pay.
The year the body never began I told you
forever it could go on this way.

8.

In conclusion it's not my job
to make anyone feel
worse about things.

Everyone has their own portion
of fear and grief to tend without
being dumped on by me.

It may chance you are a person
to whom the wealth of life
is obvious, a person

who *appreciates*. It may chance
you say I trust I will have
had been such.

34

9.

Under you the ledger shut

    and let me not evade you

Under you the sugar stirs my hand

    and let me not by grace evade you

Under you the streets continue

    and let me not by grace alone continue to evade you

Under you the reengineered eye of

    let me not evade

Under you staying watered collecting waste in small bags

    Seconds before we emerge from the tunnel, a man to
    my right crosses himself. We're vaulted suddenly onto
    a bridge, the skyline extending like a tape measure
    from its casing. I study first the northbound view and
    then the south, wondering which if either has the future
    hid in it.

Under you—*could it*—Yours,—*could it*—and saying not one
    word of my love

The Magician

I can't believe we have nervous sytems
astonishing nervous sytems
that mine speaks when you come
forthrightly or sneak up

there are sounds a violin makes
which draw across me

there are your famous goosebumps
and the hand you offer easily
as a real poet might

suspension
speaks to me in your voice
and I am floored by its continuance
your shape and heft
now that only excellence concerns me

My Pope

Down here the

Dreams of you

Have not abated

As I'd hoped.

I cannot isolate

Can't console

The appetite

That houses an

Outline mind

And belly of

You.

I drink

Cokes and speak

Your little name

And paint again,

Geometrical

Derangements

Which suck. My

Friends at least

I think love

Me, their

Faces pressed

Against my

Solitudinous

Glass, their

Landscapes

Peppered with

Children.

Can

You come. I

Really think you

Ought to come. If it

Please you I'll

Abolish all this

Language. I wish

Only an anemone

Of rampant

Nights for us,

Stars to cluster

Silently on vines.

I wish us

Infinite imaginative

Orifices to

Entertain.

A soup in the

Morning say. A

Tough cake. My

Delusion

Sustained.

I think

I thank

You for refusing

To crush me

And I don't. For

What were they

Put there, my

Pope, love,

And each

Predacious

Beauty. If I built

You a throne

To float on. If

I guessed the

One gesture to

Reduce you.

But you don't

Like it so asky

And guitarish.

Is it

My fault if it's

How I bless my

Self? Is

It my fault it's

The one bliss

I say I think

I know

How to outlast?

Dejection

I feel sorrow in the state

I haven't filed my taxes

My younger brother makes more money than me

All around people who you think should know better think the
    things that don't mean anything mean something

About character, salaries and clout, I mean, and paying your taxes

It's not that I think I was born to "flame out"

In fact I've mostly enjoyed my life

Born in another century

To a dazzling variety of privileges

Though their horizons we all must admit have soured

So what is this unbendingness in me

Which pretends to die when joined

To the real machinery of things

What truculent child

"Be sand not oil in the gears of the world"

I don't bother to write most of my poems anymore

Just think them a little and let them trail off

Like a passing arrangement of cloud

What really is the difference

To put it down and send it around

To be rejected by people who know

Nothing more about the art than I

Or perhaps be accepted to *Bullshit Sparrow Magazine*

And see the thing two years on in print or on a screen

So short, just a few lines probably

In print or on a screen so I can share it on deeper screens to be
    seen

To be doing what, exactly?

By people I barely know or respect

Isn't it nicer to let the amplitude of potential swirl within

And watch it go and leave

Like a lovely thing leaves

Rather than harness it to ego

Ride it frothing through the etched gates of

Nobody even knows where

We do it to keep each other alive

I have always believed that

But lately what keeps me alive

Is I could hardly say it

Mostly the dead I read and care for

What used to embarrass me

I love them for the shape of their days

I don't envy their cold baths and tuberculosis

But the occasional free spans of their days

As I imagine them

Legend

Mohamed Choukri

1

There were Alfred and Big Dick Dave, the blown glass apple, the pig that smiled, the woman who brought the fruit in the morning, and the girl who salvaged the peels at night. There was the writer who didn't write but lay and scoured his feet many days. There were Gun Man One and Madonna the Fist and the face lightly sketched they passed between them. Almost anything could have spoken but demurred. We revolved like an emancipated fresco, fileted dictionaries by the glib light of day. Colossally vague questions crashed through the open air among distant chirps and hammerings with unvarying frequency. Almost anything might have varied but demurred. We learned new holes, we thought to make them old. Learning was a technology of aging. Speech was a genre of sleep. Time like the Grey Cat balanced in affected stillness, then leapt toward or away always a decade or two at a time. If you didn't like one you could just wait for another. Nothing disturbed our dreaming. Intentions stormed in us, they were the point. We were good hosts when we tried, naming rocks, applying clothespins to Peter's nipples when he asked. I asked for nothing which was my way of wanting it all. Almost everyone was a designer except the Devil who was love. Pigeons raged in cages.

2

There were Cherifa and Disappointed Eunice, indolence, distance, and the fervors of taste, all rotating in the sunset's vivisected orphanage. "We must make a little space for lovers' kinks," the cactus garden seemed to suggest. We laughed and screamed when hoisted over walls. We wept in the icy stairwells we collected. Stairwells were a technology of weeping. We had never been ready for anything in our lives, we said, and we would make damn sure not to be starting now. Our expectations were studded with terrible presence. Our expectations were like tables to smoke at. Our youth was disembarking like a king, he gargled coins. "Must we always be gay and having a wretched time." Over and over, in flagrante delicto, various futures divorced us. Intentions swooned and blistered under us. They carried us: out of the house, down the steps, left at the door, right at the sand, right at the sign for haircuts, right at the cat in the box, down to the taxi stand, into the car, out onto the freeway, past the port and its jubilant fisheries, past the newly planted palms, spot-lit, past the pink apartment blocks (we liked pink), out into the green neon that only could work here. And did it? Yes, we thought it did.

3

There were tremolos at work in the Portuguese defenses. There were pornographic arias at lunch. We were policed cruelly by our moods and split one pair of crutches between us. Up and down the hill crawled the thin light's contradictory rehearsal. Woe and gin were drunk and poured again. Consider that the obstacles were static. Obstacles were a technology of feeling. Confusion was the one checkerboard regime we could afford. There were the Baron and the Prisoner, the water pails with voices, and Always Pregnant Joan who liked to sing with sailors. There were the paragraph year and the year of Pierre and the several voided satellites in nets. The void was a technology of clinging. We sampled cliffsides and regularly died. "I can't believe you won't fuck me when I'm sitting here right next to you literally in flames, grow up." She fell in love with the driver but he fell in love with Bill but Bill was selling his house at the time which he was in love with. We were tired of having ideas about France. We remembered the beach as having sand but were mistaken. Nevertheless dread leapt up to skin us, who took a handful of hexagonal naps, found we were in business.

4

There were little worlds strung as on a necklace. And the night kneeled like a leopard. There was a day his hand became familiar. And the night kneeled like a leopard. There was a kind of love like an ice block of perfume. And the night kneeled like a leopard. Our friends were gods in the old style, horny, and with a lot of petty concerns. And the night kneeled like a leopard. There was of course the weather, fat with secrets, with which we loaded letters, from which we sculpted millions of remarks. And the night kneeled like a leopard. He left the only copy in the back of a cab, it nearly killed him. And the night kneeled like a leopard. There were three or four infernal tantrums to pass between us, seated or standing, or flat drunk on our backs. And the night kneeled like a leopard. One didn't like to go home, and one never liked to leave home, or him, so they shared the tall one to have some notion of closeness. And the night kneeled like a leopard. His body, a crowd descending, his lips, an axis of heat, his eyes, bright gates in patient disrepair, went like a ferry between them. And the night kneeled like a leopard.

5

There were names you knew for what was among us. Ennui, tenderness, wretched hesitation, Luke, a paintable dish of brownish limes, mental contaminants borne on the breath, grinding machine intimacies, flat beef for example. Who brought the ice pick he killed him with? Well how the hell should we know. There were excuses nested in collapsed red genitals. There was being altogether done with ideas. You could tell the lucid agents by their ravenousness for abandoning fiestas. God bless the piggy one we liked though he kept staying lonely, gathering sands, his body strewn around in bits. Profligate glamorousness: well there you have it, had had and had been having it in fact, fifteen years of procurers, no gigantic applause. We thought the streets should be books not just more fucking pamphleture. Surely we thought the day approaches when we will not be alone, not encased in little choices, trailing bloody credit off our backs in ribbons, rushed by states away from carven immunities, hoisting a crumbling tablet onto our necks. There was not as much nudity as you might expect. Our crowns were laced with sharp paternities. Stations of experience hungered for us. We guessed we were a genre of conclusion. We hurried up.

6

There was an arena in the desert that troubled our dreams because we liked it that way. Because we liked it that way, there was Impossible Paul, seated at table with a dark and dripping kidney. There were hot mental teeth in the form of grand pronouncements. What was traced in his surmise and surgically issued traveler's cheques was so traced because we liked it that way. There was risk, a technology of progress first, and only later, an ancient brutal kindling. We were at work on elastic weaponries to assail the resistless English language. And unpoliceable zones, a manic decade, were abscesses on the culture to house us. We had that. Syllable by syllable and in spite of ourselves we fortified the tendrils of control. If I can be clear there was no answer. Picture a glittering marble held delicately up on gushing jets of viscous petrodollars, a brief and empty stint in London, a desperate stent, last-ditch, in the orifice charade. That our holes were special and contested, that the unspeakable cock at platonic love's core channeled illumination by definition in one direction we knew: the palpitating mesh, meat triangulated then primed for freedom's lash. It was why flies and greenish hazes trailed us.

7

There were children swimming in the ocean. They were provoked by growth into love. Beyond his preference for French, there was Mohamed's blue annoyance at the question, it having been posed by Sometimes Sweet Tennessee on the verge of disappearing into rampant fantasies of being eaten. Well it is good to be of good use. Germane to the epiphany pursuit were the bodies on the beach, cold occasional cases of baroque dismemberment to drink like thick sedimentary wines. "My death I simply know, Cherifa, will be grand, hand-stenciled invitations dropping like notes of a piano from my alabaster fist, my blasted personhood a pestering mist dispersed in that moment to my creditor's ledgers. It is they who shall sustain me." Sustenance was a genre of compromise to which the purest of us wouldn't stoop. They died. And in the Zoco Chico there was the standing man we fed with breakfast remnants: two green olives and a cheeseless omelet quadrant packed in a chunk of bread he waved briefly back at us when rushed with wild force by the plainclothes tourism police off the square. And there was what he had said of the food a moment before that, that God had drawn it, and my shame like a neat stack of coins God also drew.

8

There was the problem of not really being there, and its Minister Dissolving, in wig and kerchief number, under whose thumb, diminuendoing, we squirmed. There was hilariously James, though it was not per se a laughing matter, in the throes despite himself of an I alone hold the key to this wild parade parody. Though even Yves, half-entombed, was getting sick of the scraped sea, its blip of infinity, though even our sensibilities, of which there were two, had turned degenerated genres of crisis, nevertheless a fresh quiver of sodomites arrived by ferry every morning. Departure remained a meaningful machine. Arthur for example in agony was borne forever in a litter toward Marseille. In silence and Jerusalem hounded Alfred freely decomposed. For Jane, in salubrious bondage, Jane encircled by nuns with Spain to contain her, there were, interchangeably, God and the CIA. The dispatch will report we gesticulated to death, that we wanted ourselves folded, still whispering, into small leather valises. Transmission's hollow operators will have bound us fast to our enticements I bet. Fine. There was a cool stone cell beside the sky and music to roll through it. Intricate circuits of ablutions were required to approach it.

9

There was an alarm accumulating in the margin, resolve flagging in the wings. The green river, like a slender nationalism, rose. Some stayed and took their chances, went recessive, raveled days around the speaking spindle, painting bandages onto framed space. Others decamped, ground illusion down to piratico-pragmatical pyrite virtue particulate at the bleached millstone. All pastorally hedged and wept. In those fabled years, from the reaches of an open book, smaller inscrutable books were seen to rise like fresh-born islands. Like reams of irascible code, mists amassed and settled, enveloping melons and inflecting the rolling outlines of lovers. When the floor fell out of the city's name it took like a hawk to the treetops. When the well went dry we bought another one. The Mediterranean, now pinching freighters and black plumes toward the close, had interred how many thousand Californias? whose felled deserts looked blankly up from under the exit ferry on which we sipped and supped, aghast.

10

There was no way around there being no time left, if by time was meant this percolated tedium, this radiant bruise left by fruitlessness's sweet grip. And there was no necessity so to have meant it, but for those who had their hooks in you. The plague by any dry number of names already had been called toward the land, and Barbara's bodyguards disbanded. The city, believe you me, was dirty, drained, and florid. Though we continued to enjoy the meager armor afforded us there, its tomorrowishness, though we had long accommodated ourselves to its alphabet's pellucid havoc, the scratch itself was opaque and clearly fatal. A scratch. Did you really have to travel so many miles only to see it. Seeing is my heritage. For God's sake then why did you bring it here. I bring it everywhere. There was nowhere to put it down when I started out. The road was lined with monsters who called out to you in friendly tongues just to eat your body up and hold and weep over the head. I was alone and I was afraid. Well, you won't be talking your way out of this one. That's right. Square up and let loose. Back against the wall. A scratch... a scratch! For in the base of this glass, a scratch, I see a new town glimmering, a scratch, a scratch, awaiting our petty drapery, a scratch, whose oceans clank and whir.

The Crossing

The Pope is on a boat. The boat

Is on an old sea. The sea has been

Deranged by nomenclature. He

Looks into the halfburst cornflower wound

Of God's mouth in the bend of his knee.

He likes to be God's wild clacking

Abacus, His big Fish, laced with sporadic

Universals. It is supreme to be thusly

Ravaged, to know the whispered

Sugars of God's Asses, the finely flaking

Crystals of his innumerable Feet.

The Pope proposes we shall see

Rambunctious mercies unleashed as

Speculations dim in that grafted dusk

Where blood has nothing left to teach.

We must imagine our spirit as rudimentary

Therefore, as more or less a mesh

Of audacious waiting.

Revenge

plant it in my chest then the demand
the man in my absorbing cellar

his tears
broke their salt there
five hundred years

this bare divot is his name

Amatory Imitations

*But the lover is a prey to memories, and desires feed even
on his inmost marrow.*

Theocritus

I

Well, Gabriel, here I am, in full command of my powers.
    That's what the words will say. And it's true
You have to say it before you can step your foot in it.
    What should I care that you led me on for two years
Only to cut me out completely? You're choosing health
    And truly I applaud you. Though I have wished you
Constipation in my lower hours, it's the twenty-first century
    And our psychological models are crystal clear.
Only I can drag this dagger out from in between my ribs,
    No fanfare, quick and simple as trimming a cutlet.
But can I really be expected, when the bloody hole there keeps
        on talking
    To stopper up my ears, smother fascination?

II

It needs to be stated to clarify all the trouble I've been through
    That I'd hang, if I were an ancient, in marble or in bronze,
A cock like yours on every Zeus I got my faggoty hands on,
    Though I guess I'd have to be a sculptor too.

III

Tell me, James, what are you? — some kind of corpse fucker now?
    Sneaking into bed like another's man's casket, like some
Gunk-eyed half-croaked stray, stealing into kitchen trash to lick
    The dead bones clean? No self-respecting ghost humper
Needs a book to tell him they shred a little further every time.
    I'll be nicer: hot tears irrigate nothing in the pissed-out flower
        beds
Of yesteryear. Why don't you get some fresh air,
    Try it with the living for a change?

IV

Gods! If you are contented to let me debase myself as a worm,
    Sucking and chewing the mud of sweet Gabriel's absence,
Have pity and, in one divine stroke, complete this transformation,
    That I might bend myself to cry these tears directly
Into my fuckhole, and lubricate his happy coming there.

V

As my friend and contemporary Lucretius always says,
    Inside of us, we're mostly empty space. That's true, Lucretius,
And furthermore, it's our added bad luck to be Poets, bitten
        alive by the eagle
    Of not being able to let things be | in their vacuous, vast,
        disconsolate, noble silence.
No sooner does a Poet catch one whiff of the abyss than he
        commences to pour in
    Bucket after bucket of squirming words, as if bailing out his
        sailing vessel

In reverse. Well, boo-hoo to me, I'm sunk! Oh, darkly comic
     fate, to be
  A lowly singer of songs. I'd just as soon unstring this lute if,
     impossible Gabriel,
You'd come back to me. Come back to me. Put this mouth to
     its honest use.

          VI

When you're down a long time, everyone tells you to pull
     yourself together.
  Then, if it kills you, they say: "we can never know the
     sadness of another."
A lobster swims into a lobster trap and becomes a lobster. Thus
     does a lover
  Step through the jaws of love.

          VII

Oh god, oh god, oh god! Now I'm really in the shit! Never
  To smash my face again against your perfect armpit,
     unspeakable fate!
Better never to have been born! For with what paltry human
     scents must I
  Content myself, now that the sinister veil has crept between
     me, and that
One for whom my olfactory lobe was wired? Friends, I have
     stood on Olympus!
  Must I now live out my days as, what, some Humpty fucking
     Dumpty?
Oh god, oh fate: what black compost will these scattered shells
     season?

VIII

It seems to me that I am filled with nothing
   But a voracious need to suffer this.
A well at whose bottom a pair of black slow eels
   Beget themselves, ad infinitum, is me. With what
Leaping ingenuity, what muscular invention
   Does my sorrow seek and find its own occasion.
It is, I think, the knit of life's insistence itself
   Which in this way unravels me. Riddle me this,
You scholars: what will not die is killing me.

IX

He is compelled to seem almost god-like to me now
   Your new boy, Gabriel, and I can't fail to notice:
Doe-eyed, a musician, and visibly acrawl with sensitivities—
   Am I become a prototype? And does he sing you songs, sweet,
Like I once did, in my long-lost stolen storied infancy?
   It's good he should. Where you are going you will need them,
Just as I must need nothing but these gallstone verses,
   Which jet from me in crimson spurts.

X

Those whom love flows toward are well-versed
   In acts of war. With tools of war they steel
Themselves against influx; with the bludgeon
   And the catapult, the broadaxe and the mace, hurl
Absence at the elements, vent rage on space.

XI

I think about you too much. I am descended from a long line
    Of addicts. They drank too, were too unhappy
With the unhappiness that life had made them. People died,
    And the fruits of one's labors always in doubt. Then me.
You do not doubt I mean what I say, or my restraint. I doubt
    You think of it at all. Still a golden bubble in the heart
Seems preferable to stony absence, as many inebriations are
    In fact better than sobriety, though we cannot live there,
We can only die there. But we die anyway. With your name, what,
    On my lips? Ridiculous. And yet it is the wine of paradise,
Frivolous, luminous.

XII

Love gets in the way of love. There ought to be more words
    To paper the silent chamber where I've sat and watched
The moss grow over me, past hate and love, love, hate, nor that,
    Nor that one either has the breath to say
Our sadomasochistic psychosexual event now has ended.
    The spinning wheels, no, the flashing spinning top that cast
Such entrancing shadows has commenced its terminal wobble.
    I've said it before. I've said everything before.
I lower the curtain, Gabriel, and let us take a bow in the glare
    Of this totally articulated light we abandon now to its devices.
I release you to your day name and go about my business. What
      is that?
    Is where my life, uncalled for, begins, which grimaces, curls
      its tail in,
Wanders where the size of you can't follow.

Woe is me, the last human of all time, petty and godless as ever.
    I wished and wished. I was full of rote admirations
And congenially faithless. Now am I deposited without fanfare
    As a chicken's neck is simply wrung, or a napkin
Dissolves in an alley. Oh, friendless speck of heat! I can do nothing
    With or for you, not even attend your ruination. For this
Orbital skewer to speak me runs some other course's law,
    And will I think not end nor cannot end.

Here

Mezzogiorno

The beans for which
this district is named
hang in felty green gouts
from the trellis, abutted
by a shock of bamboo.
An accordion tune turns
on Sal's stereo, on repeat
a long time, pleasant still,
surprisingly
though sure to turn hellish
after an hour or so only.
The dog's name is Dollar.
The black eels in my chest
are quiet today. I read
in a tedious biography
of Caravaggio that he never made
a drawing in his life,
but cut the plan
straight into the primed canvas
with a knife. That seems
good enough. If I am not
felled by monkey pox I plan
to head south Wednesday,
swooping into baked Calabria,
skipping across Scylla
and Charybdis, and on
to Palermo, occasional capital
of the Kingdom of the Two—

you know the rest. I was too optimistic
about the accordion,
which grates already.
Have you seen Fellini-
Satyricon? "I am not
at all well in my soul,"
the first actor complains
direct to the camera
after his boy is seduced away
by a rival. There is
charisma in just saying so.
But I am well enough,
fed with incredible marmalades,
dreaming of ghastly mollusks,
playing cabana boy
with my unsteady tray of spritzes.
Now the accordion is usurped
by an innocuous pop rock ballad.
Need I even to guess
the topic of the lyric ...
Did you know my name
means Usurper? And does yours
mean simply Light? Or Clarity?
Though not all light is clear
I postulate. Some you could cut
like milk in a dish.
I'm sorry to say
the Church of Santa Chiara
in Naples underwhelmed me,
its doors blown figuratively off
by the Gesú Nuovo, baroque,
just across the way,
decked in porphyry,

with a great David in the front left corner.
I love David and antique vulgarity.
It is hot, I think,
in New York, like everywhere. I pray
you are free as I seem
to be of fits of dread
today. Now I have to go
wash dishes. XO, J

7/24/22, Frasso Telesino

Claire,

Here there are no airplanes
so the burden of distance
falls on the mountains
which I like to watch
change their faces
as globs of hours pass
me by. They start the day
full of details which
by evening bleed away
and resolve themselves
one thinks with relief
into strata of lavender
and slate. It is not
so unlike being a person—
a thought out of the old ethics
whose pages are death
to turn and in whose
drains we swirl. Have you
heard of Fra Diavolo?
I guess it's a pasta sauce
though at the end
of the 18th century
shortly before the events
of your book he led
the peasantry of this region
in guerrilla resistance against
the French. I'm told
he stayed in this villa,
with its windows shaped like eyes,
against whose door frames
I bash my German head

three times a day:
matins, nones, vespers,
ora et labora, *nec spe*
nec metu, no fear,
no hope, as Caravaggio's
motto goes.

I am acutely aware of water
and heat, alert to smoke
in the hillsides, and follow
the Italian conversation
around like an infant or a stray,
waiting on sound like meat
to squeeze some
intelligible protein from. I know
they speak of the Brothers of Italy,
and Il Dottore, a coyly mysterious guest
conducts the discussion
with gusto and authority. He's here
at work on a book
on the summer of 1943
and the bombing of San Lorenzo
in Rome where his father lived and picked
the only building on his street
to survive the blasts to shelter in.
He told me another story
but it's too gruesome for this "letter"
which you will probably read
in the morning, which is not
the time for gruesomeness.
That the times of day do matter
is the argument of this place.
It had not occurred to me

that something as old as Rome
if it were bombed
would have to be bombed
for a first time. Today is
my name day, the feast of St. James,
and a new moon
in Leo approaches.
Beware of flare ups and
the dramatic effects of exhaustion.

7/25/22, Frasso Telesino

Claire,

Today I woke up in Palermo and in a bid for freedom
shaved off my beard with an eyebrow razor.
I know, I didn't know
about eyebrow razors either.
You can buy them in the 99 cent stores here
Which of course aren't called that
here. Ah, here. Now I have a mustache.

Though I am suspending judgment
my first impression
is this is a city to die in. The streets I find
myself on all abruptly end.
From the window at my little desk
I can see the Teatro Massimo:
"the second widest theater in Europe"
says my host though surely
he must have meant something else.

I feel like a character
in an experimental early detective novel all right,
the part at the end when he discovers
he himself is the killer
his crimes committed in a ponderous haze
of laudanum withdrawal, say,
or just while he happened not to be feeling himself.
We are capable of anything
squished under memory though we be, though
Tolstoy says the bees of history impel us.

There is a staircase in this apartment
which I am constantly traversing

having left my phone or some implement
on the far side from me. My books
and underwear are all in a half-used jumble.
I can't believe you brought Shakespeare
to Italy and no clothes—that's what Dickey
says to Tom Ripley while he's being taught
to write: stars hide your fires. I say let 'em rip.

You will forgive this maudlin mood
as well as a lack of news
as it's now August
whose essence is spelled thus.

8/2/22, Palermo

Claire,

Try this: you are breathing
in blue light, the color of the sky
and exhaling the black smoke
of stupid pains in the ass.
A featureless voice guided me
through such an exercise
just now from my phone
transmuting me into a real
dragon of calm. How's that
for acts of radical modern fervor.

Perhaps we should invite
AirBnb to sponsor this epistolary
venture. They could put our pictures
on the website even, I with my
sorry mustache, you in your
luxury sewer. The tag:
take your agonies on the road.
We are just like Shelley
eating oranges on Vesuvius
in spiritual pain.

In a week I'll be back in New York,
sprinting up and down the avenues
and making snide remarks,
as we like to do there.
What will happen
between then and now
is anybody's guess. I hope
to go to the beach, and to see
the ghastly mummies

hanging on the wall here—
honestly, what is with
the catacombs? When I first
arrived in Europe every
small research I made
seemed to lead me back
to a novel instrument
of torture. The Catherine wheel
specifically somehow
I had never heard of, or
breaking wheel, or wheel
of Catherine. I bet you
already know what it is.
I won't go into it here
except to say it's named
for St. Catherine, on whom
it was meant to be used
but I think it exploded
at the mere grazing
of her saintly extremities.
Caravaggio has a painting
of her. She is leaning
toward the spike, in a
"longing for death" as
the tedious biographer
hammers out. I left that book
in the central train station
in Naples, I simply
couldn't take it anymore.
I have felt like I'm somewhat dying
all year, maybe two, but
I think this is a cheerful
process ultimately, a sacrament

of transformation
one must bear witness
and attend to. Nor do I
"long for death," but it comes,
with an upper or lower
case D, as often as
it pleases. Now look
those horrible mummies
have made me morbid.
Tell me about the next orange
thing you see, I will do
the same. Because that's life,
that's the game of being alive.

8/4/22, Palermo

Claire,

I send greetings from the small cave of my genius,
A tastefully appointed apartment on the Via Re Federico
Complete with recently restored early twentieth-century
Ceiling frescoes, not that I am looking up much,
Mostly inward, backward, and down, to keep an eye,
It goes without saying, on the armies of darkness.

Today I am tender and slight, like a delicate lettuce
About to be served to a visiting head of state. And you?
Have you figured out ser and estar? There is always
Another shade of ambiguity to be turned up
As I remember, or hacked with one's garden trowel.

Update: I have left the cave, I am just like Polyphemus
retained in legendary memory as a murderous menace
but really just trying to get along. I have made bold
to order the parmigiana and am in a craze of buying
tourist magnets for all those I could carry with me
Only as text, as little letters dancing on my phone.
Perhaps you will be so unlucky. Though my last gift
Will be hard to top.

Yes, Claire, the wind's at my back. I fly home
to my newly arrived expensive barstools
and a temporary impecuniousness which is sure to startle
but from which I'll emerge like always and always again
and the gracious arms of my loving husband and friends.

Isn't it funny to be what is called an "anxious person"?
To take to the hills or seek distant shores
simply to writhe on and seethe?

It is sobering to encounter oneself as a shucked and glistening
    oyster
aquiver at the end of an absurdly delicate fork,
but we must challenge these angels to fight
from time to time and even
like Jacob be wounded in the charge. For Jacob it was the hip.
For me perhaps my leonine pride has taken a hit, plus
whatever injury too much sugar and caffeine will wreak
and a pain in my back from not having done my stretches.

I will not let thee go unless thou bless me
we speak to the silence from naked linoleum floors.
The scholars will say I am being grandiose
but if there's another way of staying interested
I await it, as soon I will await
a train, a plane, a plane, a plane, an air train, the number 2
    subway, and later you
in inimitable New York,
where everything will be different and the same.

8/10/22, Palermo

8/31/19

I have submitted the names and contact information of three
    personal references
To the referees of death. It is looking well managed at this point.
A fine rancid mesh overlays all my concepts, the mesh is called
Having been born in the United States of America. In fact it
    was 1988.
Ronald Reagan was sitting blankly in a chair. Sex was menacing
    our nation.
The destitute and infirm had already long been having the vice
    and clamp
Applied to them and now it is thirty years later, can you
    imagine. I tell my brother
We are the worst group of people to have to learn to live smaller.
Even the most conscientious among us were born at the zenith
    of trash.
And even now our cursed and stolen acreage just sits there, so
    well insulated
Against. Give it all away, I say. I have some vegetables in the
    fridge,
An exorbitant laptop computer, and thirty or so dollars in the
    bank. One benefit
Of being rich I bet must be not doing personal math all day.
    Instead
You get to do wicked and seismic math. Numbers cradle and
    nurse you
Who are a great stupid baby with bombs and influence. From
    where I'm sitting

It's not looking so hot and that was being said before I got here.
    Meanwhile billions
Upon billions of bullets and dollars clink and whoosh in the
    night, awaiting reply.

5/8/20

rain fills the dish
a neighor leaves
nuts on
for the squirrels
on sunny days

a poet emails me
with regard to
"the sparsities to come"

cold in may today
hot in
may tomorrow

I play a part
convert
tobacco and additives
to flying cinders

Poem for Developers

you are ruining a once great city
in the name of a class of people
who can't contemplate life without a dishwasher

whose idea of a good time is a $48 Mongolian donut
on a desolate Saturday afternoon
followed by a lap at the "Museum of Crayons"
and gallons and gallons
of craft beer to convert
into craft piss

445 W. 49th St.

I was a teenage atheist in the W. Bush years
the songs were all about wanting to die though I
and my peers had been treated well by the world
all weekend we said ostensibly this ostensibly
as if a rage preempted by interlocked planks of sadness
curdled just shy of knowing a feint of rawness in its place
built of the signals of feeling it carried us off and away from

now if I say I want to die it's as if I mean to sleep
to nominally be nowhere

I don't pursue it
though every year wound around the pole is in advance
of a raveling understanding of what rest is
might be
in a world that hasn't treated you well
if by you is meant what lives
if a world is an aggrandized system of endings and not the earth
and if what's there like the poem or truth to fortify you against
        predation
is only a further betrayal
I do not know
I think it too

too easily was I born in the second to last century of malls
learned to speak and wear black there
while haywire pleasures grinned in trees out of the devious beige

to shrink to shrink
to yearn and earn
its accident like a wage

8/27/24

It smells of exhaust where I am.
The neighborhood is flooded with
children. Their fathers, in loosely
fitting Japanese-style artistic trousers,
are there to baby them, push them to
and fro in exorbitant contraptions
complete with adjustible awnings and
multiple storage compartments. Laptops
dawn. And some slobs still (thank god)
sleepwalk behind canine avatars.
Cement truck, bicycle, cement truck.
The project of progressing with increasing grace
in light of diminishing possibilities
for drastic transformation incarnates itself
buzzily, cheerfully: Morning for adults.
Morning for the dogs of America.
Do dogs jog, or go? into the horizon's
encroaching construction. What is
the drainage device affixed to baby's ear?
Delicate devilish sleepy street scene
beginning to stir, as interviewees arrive and
awkwardly hover. Jogger, biker, dogger,
kidder, cement truck mixer. Or, rather,
cement mixer truck.

3/20/21

on the first anniversary of the New York lockdown

history's toe is no marvel
no orchestra darkens its helmet
its hissing city
hisses too

discover this: this
far from sound color
retreats, a poached touch may
throb in dreams and nothing violate
the haywire exterior

well, Mary, better let it,
and elongate like a mushroom
in the rented patch
your own life's dark
for the old speeds still appall
no vicious crystals go
no feeding only talking at the trough

remember kissing
remember just sitting there

now I crack eggs, gas a roach, read, steam
like a horse in slush

Monument

Often I remember Khaled al-Asaad, scholar and archaeologist,
Who served for forty years as the principle conservator
To the remnants of the ancient citadel at Palmyra,
Who, his colleagues reported, knew its "every nook and cranny,"
Like no other person living and in a way no book could tell,
And who was tortured, when the site fell to the Islamic State,
To disclose the whereabouts of certain treasured objects
He had helped to secret away before the iconoclasts' approach.
He refused. Instead, on August 15th, 2015, at the age of 83,
He was in a public square by a masked swordsman beheaded,
His body suspended with red twine from, it was variously reported,
A traffic light in the new city, a Roman column in the old.
Often I remember this man, Khaled al-Asaad, Palmyrene,
Steadfast steward of ruins.

Large Glass Building

Here is
a large glass building.

In it a city breeds
captivating people with

interesting ideas for which they
seek a sympathetic

audience the city in
the large glass building

struggles for
some reason to produce.

They have ideas
even as to why it should be so for which

they seek the selfsame
elusive hearers.

Steeping themselves
in feeling it

works they
work thinking they

work
it, for a time as if

it were an interesting idea and not
a large glass building.

Grand Army Plaza

Someone's Beethoven dog drools crystalline ropes.
   "A Saint Bernard Newfoundland mix," his owner offers
      to those who approach. "He's a good guy." "Geez
         Louise he's huge." That's really what she said. Probably

an appropriate answer of leaves have fallen for the first
   of October. Two raincoats lead a bike to water. Pink kid
      points to me to say, "mama," excited for names. Many carry
         cups in inessential headwear. Helicopter going over which
            I always called Obama—what will I next?

Brother at work can't answer whether humans won't be as good
   at 3D, for all our screen time. Miscellaneous daily sins against
      the body I uncover daily more of, its casements and sub
         mersions. Sentences I write in cells don't scan or dis
            appoint me, though I am surprised still to be here
               always. Blue kid tosses stick from bridge: "RIP
                  stick." And the people who pick up
                  trash with the grasping tool
                  have arrived in a van
                  with Mariah.

                    In early
                  autumnal balm, fountains spray
               winding sheets o'er granite torsos black
            filmed with green. A lot of excitable
         drapery in public statuary and wing-
       bending birds of prey. Liberty not The but A
     statue of I see in flagrant cape blown back
   by the winds of Shenandoah,
Brooklyn, New York.

"Light's another enemy," they say
        holding brown bottles overhead in a tent
            where white people have gathered in rustic jackets.
            October First, long awaited day to some.

                                    And a fact, the endless
                            loop of vehicular traffic,
                        last to enter the poem.

2016

11/20/24

I like the milky quality of light in November

I like to think I'm the Roy Orbison of average American gay men

Neo-Nazis are marching in Columbus

I express a second coffee through its shining tin pod and return
    to the poem

Who does the work gets the work done

Who flees it suffers and is antic and/or morose

Orbison triumphs when my heart heaves to Crying

"I was all right, for a while"

"I could smile, for a while"

Can we see the Sienese painting show

In which long-scattered segments of admired altar pieces

Have been reunited for the first time on our continent

Tambors and timbrels of luscious color

Bent to grave themes

I want to but I can't on Monday

How are the cantons of Switzerland faring

Glacial shrinkage and "rightward drift"?

Does Canton neighbor Columbus?

Is that where he thought he was going?

45 pro-democracy activists have been sentenced to jail in
    Hong Kong

In Guangzhou a Spaniard in soft thin pants

Sliced me a tomato twelve years ago

In a dark kitchen

Whose window opened onto a thundering ten lane highway

As erotic as it sounds

New York Conversation

Fact Poem

Chimpanzees use tools.
Bowerbirds design.
Bees dance and the blue whale sings.

Reefs blanch and swoon.
Many mammals are known to scream.
All but the deathless jellyfish buy the farm.

I Think It's Sad Sometimes We Die

Sometimes I am overwhelmed by the fact of loss
Its cat eyes flashing from the corner
And I don't like to think about it
And furthermore I don't think that means anything about my
    character
Who would want to think about that

Poem in the Dominant Style

I am having sex
I am having sex with all my friends
I am having sex with all my friends

for Democracy

Tempura Fugit

watching
my neighbor's
beard grey
gradually
on Grindr

To Earn a Living Off the Language

means the cost of your labor
will cap out around
one and half burritos per hour
adjusted through the centuries
for inflation

He

he calls me the perennial beginner
when he calls

he is the tucked in flannel of lovers

Some of My Genders Summer 2019

windy room
blitzed clown
resting pebble
dead egg cup

Diary

intolerable quiet
pursued
intolerable noise

Fig Tattoo

what are you
some kind of deficient

Rich Art Kids

fresh from the cliffs
of Dover

be not accused
look
I am your language

Poem

I got a job great
I was breathing

I stretched and paid
attention

everyone blinked as if
it belonged to me

That's Wellness

skipped cycling for fear of shitting
that's wellness

Comment on the Prospect of a Career in the Arts

they're all fucking rich
especially the aggrieved ones
they're the really rich fucks

Purgatory

Eating another
Banana on steps:

Purgatory Claire
& I decide

Memo

you know
I don't mind my body

it does
basically what's asked

so unlike
me in that

Poem

I love the internet

On it my thoughts
Are almost money

Your Poems

your poems are a desolate porridge
in which accolades shine and melt

Universal Ad

sometimes it's just time
for a little something

Couplet Composed During the New York Blackout of 2019

If I can't have you soon
I shall die, which is fun.

The New Masculinists

ape ardor

they've rediscovered
blood

heroically
they burn down
the house we live in

*After Writing Some Poems I'm Not Sure I Like After a Long
Time Writing Nothing*

I will let them be a little bland now
like makeshift meals
in an unfamiliar kitchen

Long Island Railroad

So. On a train beside a dozen
Pale yellow roses. Wax pale but
Freely interspersed

With tiny white frill, many
Little heads
Dreaming treason. And the green

Cupping them in arrowy
Outline, flat against
The plastic cradling all.

The open and organic markets
Are for me. There you are
For me.

A dirty window I
Watch flaxen light at, the brownish
Crowns I see

Entangled with stellar midi
Warble announcing
Announcing. Shoes also

Brown
And a split-open
Thumb incurred

Resolving a bookcase yesterday
On not-Easter. Life is the dream
of arising from natural torpor

For some, defying
The vapid statue-laden
Factories, their brutal chutes, their powdery

Grass in clusters.
And though we are without
The dream of flying backwards, the light

Does if you want it to
Smile (grin?) on the silver car park.
Outward facing frame!

You leaving roses
Alone while you stagger
In the moving bathroom compartment,

Unfelt joy
Of trust and balance, intricate
Gridwork of spiritual

Escape, support today
Washed hair and softening denim.
Then the diva turn,

The red one letter
Offers its
Graspable arc.

Think on topics.
Pack a bag.
How

Though you
Are here
I miss you.

Paumanok

of dreams today
is the 8:25am train
from Chicago Union
Station to Milwaukee

honeys desiccating among first umbers
late greens, fits of pink, bare elms

and all my life is here
is difficult
gentle, and forgives me

An Oblique Portrait of Garrett Phelps in 2023

extracted from a journal of that year

Afterward Garrett cashes us out and we go to Sharlene's where Asshole Tom is working.

Then Matvei and Garrett arrive and we begin to rearrange the space, unpacking an enormous shelf and moving things back and forth. Lots of climbing up and down onto chairs, using the drill, etc.

Garrett arrives and we order a car and bring the table downstairs and chat on the ride over and I learn he's a translator, translating Oswaldo Lamborghini of all people who I was just thinking maybe I should translate some short days ago. Isn't that funny we think.

Then I walk to Rachel's to get her studio keys having loaned mine out to Garrett last night which she's left in a little plastic baggy behind the lockbox attached to a Palm Springs keychain.

Make it to studio by 10 to meet Garrett Phelps for his Wednesday of work.

I drop Garrett a set of keys and walk the box to the studio, stopping for a little grocery store sushi.

Then studio around 10. Garrett arrives too but can't quite manage the keys, sorry Garrett. I show him how.

Arrive quite grumpy at work. Garrett is already there talking to Matvei. Hi Matvei. How was your trip. Great but now I'm back. Then I sit at my desk and try to work while Garrett does his work. He retrieves an enormous roll of plastic wrap from the mailroom. It's the size of a monster truck tire. We're aghast.

Text Garrett that I am coming but I'm moving slow.

Garrett also turns up at some point and brings some boxes up into the space.

Garrett shows up at some point.

But today is a productive day. I hit the perfect slot machine combination of caffeination and am supercharged, accomplishing thousands of tasks while Garrett works at his computer. It's go, go, go. I feel great! If only every day were like this.

When we get back I shove my way to the back where Garrett is selling books and listen to the readings.

Aiden and Garrett and the whole Litmus crew are all in the studio, including Elizabeth Willis who is working on the book of witches.

Garrett couldn't get his shift covered at the bookstore so I am subbing in as bookseller.

Elina and Garrett are not to be found but we prepare ourselves some bourbon on ice and sit in the backyard in the dark under bright stars.

By now we've left the bar and stop for "Sonoran hot dogs." All the young people are wearing hip high silver boots. The dogs are great. Chris says "that's just how it is." Then walking generally homeward he wants to play a song from his punk days on my phone called BIG DICK. Garrett is trying to roll me a cigarette but failing miserably. Back at the house we each pour ourselves a pint of bourbon as a night cap and sit outside and dutifully sip it before we realize it's really the end of the line for us, pouring it all into one big cup so as not to waste it, and proceeding to put our drunk asses to bed.

We realize we're hungry and Garrett and I buy weird bowls of food.

She has a job interview at 4 and so we eat the burritos and chat some more and then she's off and I walk up to the studio where Garrett. I came in to write in my journal and in theory maybe catch up on some freelance work but I don't do that, I mostly help Garrett who is battling the printer which is smudgily printing all the labels he needs.

I hug her. Garrett is selling books. I am feeling bedraggled by it all.

Garrett shows me an outlandish copy of *Wuthering Heights* with a bizarre cover illustration of a man with windswept (we theorize) hair.

And most of my friends are gone by now, and most of the bar's patrons generally, but I sit at a little table with Garrett and Ely and the girl who bought me a shot for my birthday.

Garrett is here and we talk about New Years' plans. He said his might turn out "rather gay." Good for you I say. The gays know how to party.

Complaint

And if hummingbirds with drones on them to use with our
    touchscreen technologies

And if get them out of my face

And if they need to relax about that

And if you stopped taking days off we could afford the fucking bed

And if it's not the one for you

And if she didn't realize

And if people should think about how much coffee they drink in
    the morning before criticizing my drug habit

And if the whole city should be a park employing its citizens to
    walk around and generate buzz

And if the real reason is he feels ambivalent about the way that
    moving on would be a kind of betrayal of his pain

And if well that's not his job

And if art were just a planetary feedback loop would that be so bad

And if the sewers don't last the storm

And if I find your attempt to blend an overall Swedish space
    station aesthetic with rustic colonial accents problematic or
    if just ugly am I still conclusively not a fan

And if you should stop hate-spending money with people who
    give you aggravations

And if his fake non-profit idea is very stupid

And if they'll wait for you out there somewhere you reasonably
    could find them

And if they want to be seen

And if the bridge holds and all the heavenly promises come back
    under budget

And if our lives will be returned to us in breach of contract

And if my wish to carve a hole out of each day in which to
    deposit some rations for the journey back will not have
    been in vain

And if we will collect collect collect

6/21/20

it's father's day

my back spasm he relates is an ancestral affliction

he himself has also spasmed as had his father before him

our trunks are too long for our legs there's a word for it

and I died in an explosion in two friends' dreams this week

well, I tell them separately, don't really love that

in another's special lobsters have crept in through the window

I'm there to tell him to "bonk" them on the head

I don't tell him I think the dream means the monsters of
    my unconscious

have infested his personal space I don't have to

it's the third week of the fireworks' infiltration the second
    of three eclipses

the summer solstice my half-birthday and the second day
    of this poem

meanings are slathered everywhere like a rich excess of butter

on the plain puck-like bread of experience for now

Tornare

It's this wrestling with you
Sharpening my wits
Throwing up my hands
A smile there again behind the door
"Whoever you love that's who you love"

I don't doubt your goodness
Your quick hands prune the tree of its diseases
Then to express creature joy in the buds rebounding
Creature joy is inalienable goodness
And alienable I
Doubt and dress it up as
Thirty-five-hundred mornings melt
Into a throb my capacity to lose
A shining
Thing of such imagining is all I

You would find this silly
You have understanding
I have the mind's hectic business
So that I may return I roam
To know my love you
Like a home with no doors and no curtains
Nothing to trap or hide
And where even the fuzz of mental strife
Can know rest and be kindly known

I'm only a nervous man
But I outwit him
Steal from under the king's eye

A moment's kiss
A piece of toast
Summer's feet gone cold
And warmed again

Illustration

the carrots planted
to withstand the cold
spring rotted because
it was a wet spring

they rotted

the laundry on the line
was strung out
to dry but did the
opposite, besoaked
itself when the rain
began to fall itself
in fat green drops

that's what happened
to the carrots and
the laundry

that's their story

swallowing up intentions
they swelled

Work Space

for Steven Dean

These spectacular escarpments yield

a sordid lineage, rife with the bliss

of some meticulous collision.

What a disaster! This passive gore

perspectivized beyond all cringing:

that is how art flays the dust off

any easy day, forces a pretty hat

to play the icicle that nonsense

might withold. Try on a new context:

open types, fleece and gourd, a teeming

sill to quell a dark meat wish. You

don't always find such personally

meaningful contractions, and who

cares? Purples retire. Corkboards

lean into pricking. Practice squinting

and this sordid lineage yields

a frigate-flower, though some trails are

reserved for VIPs. "The dog goes pinkly

blooming past peripheral dialects

like a tomato stuck with pins," or

"wow I keep pens forever."

Meticulous collisions yield a road

out of foreclosure. Bundle discursion,

pack a bag for the cathedral.

Extending soundscapes scrape spectacular escarpments like

"What a great space," troubles yielding

like marimbas, some post-its to initiate

pursuit. Steven, I tried it open. What followed

closed. We tape at cracks in walls, mix

toothpaste plasters. Art sprays a future dust

on passing glass to make it better,

compromised glitter by which we are

foresworn. I aim my mirror, hunker down

and memory unfurls a field of hooks

we glide beyond, as an autoroute

tells love's imploded motive—well, just that

he who sleeps in my backseat that man is my friend

and these castellated truisms and phony obligations

egde a parting dust. They toss us up, as

clocks shock and parse us, as every pace

confirms a certain version of our depth.

A human noise snakes the gorge, sees how

landscapes evanesce against your delicate

tumult who are my church beyond all yawning

tender jests recoup disperse.

Wager

unequivocally a sissy

strong

perpendicular

with no illusions but

the one big one

one must sacrifice

the small ones to afford

to perform

do that for us won't you

too much money in the bank

impedes speech

and guilt is not

compelling compulsory

but only sits there

sour

inwardly flaking

the imagining

of huge immobile stones

any day

resolve not to

fear loneliness

which irrigates

all love's greenery

contextualizing

touch though feel

free to continue

to resent pain's

mundane encroachments

in fact

it is good

to have a little bitterness

to coax and toy with

everyone I think

secretly loves it

respects

the surly housecat

the true spur

at the heart

of placid rectilinear

eagerness

that is my wager

and as sound

a one as any

I put this moment here

April 2021

why call the light back
to sit in its shattery errand
like a corporate piece of pottery
shoved into the sun

what bribe brings its darts on even
which pierce such fancy questions from me

*

pain is plain occasion little tongue
don't be opaque
and leaving what you can of it behind

*

every season breaks your heart
that's what they're there for
hearts, the heart of the forms of appearances
cracking on its heel and
echoing down a bungalow bathroom mirror
old sad face of a man
me, my man, say I

in many a future contented
in sad ones all men

                        *

what study of love again gunned down around me
what tether
what slow air structured in the blood

what slow
you drunk in violet grass wouldn't
answer me

answer me
wouldn't

cover my eyes with your answer

                        *

too little
to fill, to
follow

fallow

is the
night not
understanding

                        *

I put this moment here
I leap like a flea from grief

                        *

the end of endlessness where
the foam of self sifts off
is rife with bells nevertheless

old claims
dwindling prisms

*

some pains point
others sink and line the base

in aerials and dim arrays obscure others
decline gesture

out of minor sunlight
hatches power
we learn in time to lose

*

a ziggurat of knowing nothing
crowns the scar of intellect
I too have told too many lies
I too am skewered by design
it's serious business, mercy
evasion, playing
the baffled inlet where
in blobs of wistful sputum
this soft strife's crossed days break
not one belligerent handbook
to tell why the little fire
for you in me could scour and skin a world entire

*

I put this moment here
to station myself in the way of life

a common vowel
privately incorporated

the lake is high
and unalone

a pinprick
a pain small enough to crawl through

o
season of the hole's precedence
unmaking maker
carry us alongside love's rough infancies
just long enough

Acknowledgments

Thank you to Claire DeVoogd, Abby Dring, Will Fesperman, Stacy Skolnik, Andrew Stone, Rachael Wilson, and Matvei Yankelevich for reading and commenting on prior versions of this book with generosity. Thank you to Ry Cook and Aiden Farrell for a consequential invitation to read at Unnameable Books. Thank you to my poetry teachers: Jan Ledman, Michael Hofmann, Julie Agoos, Ben Lerner, Marjorie Welish, and Anselm Berrigan. Thank you to Ely Watson, Rachael Wilson, Miriam Atkin, Öykü Tekten, Anselm Berrigan, Tom Haviv, Emily Bark Brown, Zoe Tuck, and Keith Newton, who first published sequences or poems from this book in a manner detailed as follows: "Mezzogiorno" as a chapbook by SLAB; "Amatory Imitations" as a chapbook by Most Perfect World / Pinsapo; "Grand Army Plaza" in *Brooklyn Rail*; "Saturn" in *Kaf*; "My Pope" in *Hot Pink*; and "3/20/21" and "11/20/24" in *Harp & Altar*.

"Legend" was commissioned by Than Hussein Clark for his exhibition *A Little Night Music (And Reversals)* which showed at CRAC Occitanie. Thank you to Than for the invitation. "Legend" (as *The There Poems*) and "I put this moment here" were first published as chapbooks by Terrific Books.

JAMES LOOP is a writer from Central New York and the author of several chapbooks. His work has been published in the *Brooklyn Rail*, *Hot Pink*, *Hyperallergic*, *Lambda Literary*, and *Prelude*. Audio/visual iterations of poems have been exhibited at Art-o-rama (Marseille), CRAC-Occitanie, Frieze London, and the Material Art Fair (Mexico City). For Belladonna* Collaborative, he has curated readings at Brooklyn Museum, Brooklyn Public Library, Montez Press Radio, and elsewhere. He lives in Brooklyn and works as the Publicity Director for World Poetry. *Metronome* is his first full-length poetry collection.

Metronome
Copyright © James Loop, 2026

ISBN 978-1-959708-19-3

First Edition, 2026 — 1400 copies

Winter Editions, Brooklyn, New York
wintereditions.net

Library of Congress Control Number: 2026932091

Distributed by Asterism Books (US) and Public Knowledge (UK).

Typeset in Heldane, a renaissance-inspired serif designed by Kris Sowersby for Klim Type Foundry, and Zirkon, a contemporary gothic designed by Tobias Rechsteiner for Grilli Type. Design based on series templates developed in consultation with Andrew Bourne.

This book was printed and bound in Lithuania by BALTO print with Munken papers. Manufactured by Arctic Paper in Sweden, Munken meets EU Ecolabel, Forest Stewardship Council, and Cradle to Cradle certification standards.

WE is grateful for the support of our subscribers, and extends special thanks to recent Supporting and Lifetime Subscribers: Anonymous (2), Anonymous (in memory of the Beaubiens), Yevgeniy Fiks, and Katy Lederer.

WE is a member of the Community of Literary Magazines and Presses (CLMP) and of Poetry Corp., a publishing cooperative. Tax-deductible donations are much appreciated and should be made through our fiscal sponsor, Ether Sea Projects, Inc.

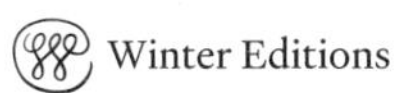 Winter Editions

Emily Simon, IN MANY WAYS

Garth Graeper, THE SKY BROKE MORE

Robert Desnos, NIGHT OF LOVELESS NIGHTS, tr. Lewis Warsh

Richard Hell, WHAT JUST HAPPENED

Marina Tëmkina & Michel Gérard, BOYS FIGHT

Claire DeVoogd, VIA

Monica McClure, THE GONE THING

Ahmad Almallah, BORDER WISDOM

Hélio Oiticica, SECRET POETICS, tr. Rebecca Kosick

Heimrad Bäcker, DOCUMENTARY POETRY, ed. & tr. Patrick Greaney

Robert Fitterman, CREVE COEUR

Karla Kelsey, TRANSCENDENTAL FACTORY: FOR MINA LOY

Alan Gilbert, THE EVERYDAY LIFE OF DESIGN

Betsy Fagin, FIRES SEEN FROM SPACE

Cristina Pérez Díaz, FROM THE FOUNDING OF THE COUNTRY

Sarah Riggs, LINES

Leah Flax Barber, THE MIRROR OF SIMPLE SOULS

Monique Wittig, THE LESBIAN BODY, tr. David Le Vay

Monique Wittig, ACROSS THE ACHERON, tr. David Le Vay with Margaret Crosland

Nathalie Quintane, THE CAVALIER, tr. Jonathan Larson

Serena Solin, A BARER SKY

James Loop, METRONOME

Jacqueline Waters, THE FRY

Iliassa Sequin, QUINTETS, ed. Luke Roberts

Keith Newton, REVOLUTIONS AMONG US

Jean Day, THE ELEMENTS

Rodrigo Toscano, SALVAGE NATION

POSTCARDS OF THE SIEGE: VISUAL CULTURE DURING THE SIEGE OF LENINGRAD (1941–1944), ed. Polina Barskova

Vasily Kamensky, TANGO WITH COWS, tr. Eugene Ostashevsky, ed. Daniel Mellis